What Our Readers Have Said...

"Although I consider myself a seasoned sales professional, it is helpful to have past learning's refreshed. The books were also beneficial because of the information concerning 'trends' in the sales relationship. The sales process should be viewed as dynamic since business relationships change regularly."

•

"For the particular business I am in and the type of sales calls I have, I find that the books in the Pinpoint Sales Training Series are very often applicable to how I conduct business. I would recommend them to other sales people, just not ones that are in my industry."

•

"These books provide very good concepts. It fits in well with the Bell Leadership training program that I attended in November."

•

"I use this material in these books and apply it to my customers and other employees I work with."

•

"I would like to know other topics. Is there anything on Production Management or Consultative Selling or Time Management?"

•

"These books are great tools that should be used as guidelines for our ev-

eryday supervisory practices. You need to take the time to do a short self-evaluation when reading them."

•

"The Pinpoint Training Series delivers information that could be used in a lot different areas."

•

"I like this because I can take them with me to read at a convenient time. I feel the little time I have to spend in the office is best use on activities that directly relate to revenue opportunities. I like the short amount of time it takes to keep up with these."

•

"I prefer the self-study approach; it fits in with my schedule."

•

"My thought is that the real value of these books comes into effect when doing the action plans."

•

"Short and sweet. These books are easy to comprehend."

•

"I have enjoyed reading these books. They are relevant to today's work environment and the ongoing change in the way we manage our workforce."

•

"I do feel that these books have been very helpful to me at my job."

•

"I think a lot of the recommendations in these books are very useful, and can be applicable to everyday situations. If nothing else, it's a good reference guide to fall back upon if a situation arises in the future."

•

"These books are relevant to today's work environment and the ongoing change in the way we manage our workforce."

•

Prospecting

Pinpoint Sales Skill Development Training Series

TIMOTHY F. BEDNARZ

MAJORIUM
BUSINESS PRESS

Pinpoint Sales Skill Development Training Series
"Prospecting"
Timothy F. Bednarz

Graphic design: Monika Pawlak

Majorium Business Press
2025 Main Street
Stevens Point, WI 54481
715.342.1018 • 800.654.4935

ISBN 978-1-882181-44-5

Printed in the United States of America

Introduction

The Pinpoint Sales Skill Development Training Series is designed for targeted training and education regarding increased improvement in a specific skill or competency.

Each book within this series is designed to be easy to use, understand and apply to your job. It can be used as a basis for training individuals, as a discussion guide or as a personal training tool.

Each chapter within this book discusses a specific concept. When you have completed all eight chapters you should have a 360° perspective of the topic.

Additionally, each chapter is divided into specific sections:

- The first section provides you with an overview of the topic
- The Implications section discusses why the concept is important, and why it is important to learn and apply.
- The Strategies, Tips & Techniques to Apply section teaches how to use and apply the particular concept to your work.
- The Points to Ponder section gives you something to think about or to be discussed with a group setting. These are questions not meant to be immediately answered, but to be pondered over time.
- The Training Activity section provides you with the tools to transfer what you have learned to your job. It is designed to help create an action plan to effectively apply the concept.

Each of the topics in this series is time-tested and proven in the marketplace. They have been used by thousands of employees as training tools. Many of the users have commented that what made these books valuable, was the ability to refer to them when a problem surfaced. They indicated that they remembered reading about the exact problem. They referred back to these books and found an appropriate solution.

You will find them equally valuable as a resource in your professional development library.

Table of Contents

LEARNING OBJECTIVES:

- The reasons behind prospecting.
- Identify and develop prospects.
- To develop a prospecting strategy.
- To determine how to qualify a prospect.
- To develop a prospect into a customer.

1

Before You Prospect, You Must Suspect

Many salespeople view prospecting and cold calling as one in the same. Before a salesperson cold calls there should be a pre-qualified prospect. This maximizes his or her time and minimizes overall frustration.

Prospecting is a system of intelligence gathering that maximizes the salesperson's time and efforts by identifying the "most likely suspects" and pre-qualifying them as prospects.

IMPLICATIONS — WHAT THIS MEANS TO YOU

While some salespeople consider the terms synonymous, there is a distinct difference between cold calling and prospecting. Many salespeople begin to cold call without first identifying the most logical prospects to call on. They comb an office building or industrial park, hoping for the best. This often results in wasting their most valuable resource—their time.

There must be a "suspect" before there can be a prospect. Cold calling is an exercise in futility until a prospect is identified. The best use of time includes identifying the most probable suspects and doing the research to determine if they are realistic prospects. While this may seem time-intensive, it will actually reduce the overall time required to take the prospect through the sales process while minimizing wasted calls on companies with no interest in the salesperson's product or service.

STRATEGIES, TIPS & TECHNIQUES TO APPLY

Prospecting is a precise intelligence gathering system that needs to be strictly adhered to. With no way to shortcut the process to achieve sales success, the steps to follow include:

Profiling

The first step in prospecting is to develop a profile of the ideal prospect. Information and criteria to be developed on the prospect includes the industry, company type, application, usage and target product. Once an ideal profile has been created, parameters need to be established to provide an acceptable range for each of the specified criteria. Since most prospects will not fully meet the criteria for the ideal, the salesperson should identify the prospects that fall into their targeted ranges.

Depending upon the breadth of the product line, the salesperson may need to develop profiles for each of his or her major products.

Targeting

The second prospecting step involves identifying potential companies by industry and company type that meet the salesperson's profile criteria. This develops an initial pool of potential candidates for the salesperson to filter through.

Suspecting

The salesperson will filter through their pool of suspects by applying the specific criteria created by their profiles. This step creates a filtered pool of candidates for them to work on. However, a candidate is not a prospect until further research is conducted to pre-qualify them as such.

Researching

Research and comparing the suspect company against the targeted profile allows the salesperson to pre-qualify the suspect and convert them into a prospect. When they fit the established parameters, they have been qualified as a prospect.

Additionally, research identifies the initial needs of the company, the probable decision maker, and pinpoints problems, issues, competition and a host of other information the salesperson needs to properly approach the prospect.

Identification

The final step is to confirm the research and identify the ideal prospects for the salesperson to work on. By following this system salespeople have not only identified the most likely prospects, but adequately prepared to immediately and intelligently discuss the prospect's needs and probe for the less obvious needs.

Salespeople often find they are able to perform several of these steps simultaneously once they become acquainted with the system.

POINTS TO PONDER — SOMETHING TO THINK ABOUT

1. How have you prospected for new business in the past? Did you employ an intelligence gathering system or did you "wing it?"
2. How successful have your prospecting efforts been in the past? What factors do you attribute to your success or failure? Explain.

TRAINING ACTIVITY — APPLICATION & ACTION PLAN

Develop a target profile for your ideal customer. If you have several major products, develop one for each.

1. Identify the industry, customer type, usage, application, volume and sales potential.

2. Identify any additional criteria that you feel are important when describing your ideal prospect.

2

Developing a Prospecting Strategy

The gold prospectors of yore took the time to scout out the terrain and identify the most promising location to mine for gold. They took certain criteria into account before they made their final decision. Then they took the time to work their claims. The sales term "prospecting" derives its meaning from these early gold prospectors. The salesperson needs to develop a strategy and look over the terrain until they find the most promising area to pan for their "gold."

IMPLICATIONS – WHAT THIS MEANS TO YOU

Many salespeople don't understand what it takes to genuinely prospect their territories for new business. For many, driving around to physically identify a prospect, thumbing through the phone book or going on the Internet is the maximum extent to which they will prospect. However, successful prospecting entails salespeople identifying the type of prospect they are searching for, then using all available resources to identify where that specific prospect may be located. The old prospector knew what signs to look for. A successful salesperson also knows how to identify the signs or criteria that point the way to new business.

Just as it took the old prospector time to work their claim, it takes today's salesperson time to work their territory to develop the best prospects for their business.

STRATEGIES, TIPS & TECHNIQUES TO APPLY

To achieve the desired results, salespeople must have a prospecting strategy they can follow. A well-defined strategy should be adaptable and based upon actual experience. The blueprint for a basic prospecting strategy includes the following steps:

Establish a Goal

A strategy or a plan without an established goal is as useful as a ship without a rudder. The salesperson will wander aimlessly looking for new business prospects in every nook and cranny with minimal results. It is better to have a well-defined goal that identifies a specific industry or niche and to work it until it is completely developed. Only then does the salesperson move on to the next prospecting area.

Prioritize Products and Markets

Some salespeople sell a well-defined product line to specific niche markets. However, many are selling a broader line of products. Salespeople need to identify their key products and prioritize them according to the highest sale and profit potential. The best prospecting strategy is to focus like a laser on one specific product area at a time. Once salespeople have identified and prioritized each of their products, they can focus on the product or product group deemed to have the highest priority.

Profile the Target Prospect

Once the product or product area has been defined, the salesperson will need to profile the target prospect. Normally this will be done by type of industry, company and application. Secondary criteria would include sales potential, profitability and usage. In some industries, salespeople might target companies that operate certain types of equipment as additional criteria for their products. The final profile will be used to identify and filter sources of information later in this process. The important thing is the salesperson now understands specifically who they are looking for, making prospecting much easier.

Determine Geographic Boundaries

Many salespeople have predetermined sales territories with established boundaries. Other salespeople might be covering larger geographic areas, in which case they should determine the geographic boundaries of their prospecting. They may want to create several prospecting sectors and then devote their efforts to one area at a time. The objective is to maximize results by conducting a search in manageable portions.

Identify Informational Sources

The best source of prospects is found in networking with other salespeople and business sources. The second best source of information is the Internet. By creating a target profile, it is relatively easy to search the Internet using the profile as the search criteria. Not only will an Internet search identify a prospect, but it is also a valuable source of information to be used to develop a sales approach and strategy.

In addition to these effective sources of information, there are other more conventional sources, including phone books and industry, association and trade directories. However, most of these sources of information are also readily accessible on the Internet.

Filter the Information

Once the source of information is identified, it is easy to apply the criteria developed in the target profile to filter through the information and identify the most likely prospects. This effectively serves to pre-qualify the prospect.

Contact

The final step of prospecting is to make the initial contact with the prospect. This is a hand off from prospecting to cold calling, which requires a completely different set of skills.

It should be noted that a salesperson can conduct several prospecting plans simultaneously. However, each search should have a well-defined strategy and profile to follow.

POINTS TO PONDER — SOMETHING TO THINK ABOUT

1. What techniques have you employed to develop new business leads for your territory? How successful have you been? Explain.
2. When you prospect, do you use a target profile or do you just look for any possible business you can find?

TRAINING ACTIVITY — APPLICATION & ACTION PLAN

1. Utilizing the seven-step blueprint identified above, create a prospecting strategy for your territory.
2. Identify and prioritize your major products or product groups and create a target prospecting profile.
3. Once developed, implement this strategy.

3

Identifying and Classifying Prospects

Most salespeople tend to think in linear terms when they approach prospecting. They are looking for the largest pool of potential customers they can find using the traditional "A-B-C-D" approach to classifying accounts by sales volume. This lack of creativity limits the salesperson's thinking and their sales potential.

IMPLICATIONS – WHAT THIS MEANS TO YOU

When competition intensifies and the economy slows, salespeople must use every available resource—the most valuable of which is their own creativity.

Most salespeople are singularly focused on the next sale. They fall into the comfort zone of the selling system they know, typically the sales track method of selling, which while outmoded is practiced by over 80% of all salespeople. Additionally, salespeople normally sell the products they are told to sell to the type of accounts they are told to sell to. Most fail to get "outside of their box" and creatively expand their sales horizons. The salesperson who does, holds a dramatic competitive advantage.

STRATEGIES, TIPS & TECHNIQUES TO APPLY

As previously stated, most salespeople will tend to classify their prospects based upon sales volume and subsequently attempt to fit them into a preconceived box of companies they should sell. However, there are more creative ways to identify and classify prospects, including:

Application

Numerous companies in different industries may have similar applications. These companies may be located in industries that the salesperson has not considered to be viable sources of business. As technology continues to drive new business advancements, salespeople must take the time to view their products from different perspectives. Constantly thinking of other potential applications they may not have previously considered, they must network with other salespeople to keep informed of the changes in a variety of different industries that may have a use for their product or service in a new application. This includes talking with other salespeople within their own companies to determine if they are doing something new with their product line.

Product Use

Product usage is closely aligned to application, with some minor differences. Application looks at a similar application of a product or service in different industries. Product use looks at the product to supply different applications. In many cases the application might remain the same, but when prospecting, the salesperson must look for new and potential uses for their products in places they have previously ignored.

Machine or Equipment Use

In many instances, the products sold by a salesperson work well on specific types of machines or equipment. In these situations, salespeople need to closely ally themselves with sales representatives from the specific machine or equipment manufacturer who can identify just where existing equipment has been installed and where new installations are scheduled. If a strong enough relationship exists, these people can refer the salesperson to such accounts. They can also recommend the salesperson's product to maximize the performance of their own product.

Industry

Viewing prospects by industry is a more conventional approach. However, when this perspective is cross-referenced with the three previous application criteria and product and machine use, the salesperson's insight into who constitutes potential customers may appreciably change.

Company Type

Company type is a subset of application. Once the salesperson has identified all possible applications, the second step is to identify the company types as potential prospects.

This is a conventional method of classifying prospects, but many salespeople limit this perspective by the expected company types they sell to or the ones they are expected to sell.

Sales Potential

Sales potential is the most common method used by salespeople when attempting to identify a prospect. While it is a valid approach, sales potential should be used as a filter when pre-qualifying a prospect and not as a primary determining criterion.

Cross Referencing

The most powerful approach to prospecting is to cross-reference all six of the criteria listed above. The salesperson should create a prospecting matrix listing the criteria across the header and the potential prospects down the margin. Time should be taken to study this matrix and analyze it for trends and patterns that lead to new sources of potential business.

POINTS TO PONDER — SOMETHING TO THINK ABOUT

1. What has been your approach to prospecting? What primary criteria have you used to identify prospects?
2. Can you think of new applications or places where your product can be used that you have not considered before? Explain.

TRAINING ACTIVITY — APPLICATION & ACTION PLAN

Using Excel or a simple sheet of paper, create a prospecting matrix listing the six criteria (Application, Product Use, Machine Use, Industry, Company Type, Sales Potential) across the top.

1. Along the side identify your major accounts and classify them using the six criteria listed. Examine for trends and patterns.
2. Begin to identify potential prospects and classify them using the six criteria. Examine for trends and patterns.
3. Cross-reference your existing business against your prospecting list. Examine for similarities and differences. Attempt to gain insight into where new business opportunities may lie.
4. Create a series of "what if" statements that you can apply to your matrix that can identify potential sources of new business.

4

The Importance of Preparation When Prospecting

Too many salespeople approach appointments with the attitude that prospects are there to educate them about their business—and are quickly shown the way to the door. With a wealth of informational resources available at their fingertips, there is no reason for a salesperson to be ill-prepared when approaching a new prospect.

IMPLICATIONS — WHAT THIS MEANS TO YOU

Customers and prospects expect salespeople to possess a degree of expertise in their industry, customers, products and services that they themselves do not possess. The salesperson who fails to recognize this reality is doomed to fail. The contemporary salesperson is an information manager, not the peddler of wares of days past. They are expected to manage the data and information at their fingertips to provide their customers and prospects with sound and applicable knowledge. In today's environment managers are awash in information and starving for knowledge.

As a salesperson prospects for new business, they should use their information management expertise to develop a base of knowledge they can use not to sell a prospect, but to help them improve their business. Preparation requires the salesperson to identify key issues and problems that a prospect may be facing and to identify possible solutions that help them to resolve these issues. The approach of asking a prospect to tell them about their business is a poor one.

STRATEGIES, TIPS & TECHNIQUES TO APPLY

Salespeople should know prospects are not responsible for educating them in all the particulars of their business. In fact, it is the salesperson's expertise and experience that earns them the right to see the prospect. If the prospect can't immediately identify a compelling reason as to why they should give a salesperson their valuable time, it is highly unlikely they will ever be able to get an appointment to make a sales presentation.

When a salesperson conducts a basic background investigation of a prospect's company, they are able to glean some of the key issues and problems facing the company, discuss them intelligently and offer some preliminary solutions to spark interest. This immediately separates the salesperson from the rest of the competition and greatly increases the likelihood of gaining access.

Additionally, the more knowledge a salesperson has about a prospect, their business and their key issues and concerns, the faster trust and rapport is established. An intelligent discussion about their business, needs and concerns is far superior to a salesperson who glances around the prospect's office looking for something upon which to base small talk.

Pre-qualifying a prospect by investing time in research enables the salesperson to determine if there is a real need, if the prospect can afford the product being offered and whether they are in a position to acquire it. Pre-qualifying a prospect through research allows the salesperson to spend their time identifying their true needs and developing an appropriate solution. This also eliminates many objections that typically arise due to inadequate qualification.

Prospects have little patience for the unprepared salesperson. Their time is too valuable to teach them about their business. Investigative prospecting not only identifies the prospect, but also provides the salesperson with the tools they need to approach them intelligently and offer a solution that sparks their interest and demonstrates professionalism.

POINTS TO PONDER — SOMETHING TO THINK ABOUT

1. How much do you typically prepare for your initial contact with a prospect? Does time play a critical role in your preparation? When and where?
2. What results did you experience in the past based upon the amount of preparation you invested? Explain.

TRAINING ACTIVITY — APPLICATION & ACTION PLAN

Determine the following information for a primary prospect you have identified:

- Problems
- Key issues
- Industry trends affecting them
- Potential solutions
- Three compelling reasons based upon this information why the prospect should consider your offer

5

The Best Prospecting Approach

Each salesperson will approach prospecting from a different perspective. Prospecting is a skill more suited to a police detective than a salesperson, but it is an essential skill to nurture.

How a salesperson prospects can range from the mundane to the creative with varying results. Any approach, provided it is well executed, will produce results. An effective but poorly executed approach will produce minimal results.

IMPLICATIONS — WHAT THIS MEANS TO YOU

Most salespeople have a genuine disdain for prospecting. It goes against their grain: salespeople are active individuals who want to get out and interact with their customers. They are results-driven and focus seriously on their priorities.

Effective prospecting is an activity that yields results over the long-term, but is nonetheless very boring to most salespeople. Most will only think of it when their numbers drop. Successful salespeople understand the value of keeping their pipeline full of prospective business. To do this, they include active prospecting as part of their sales lives. By never ceasing to prospect, their activity levels remain high and the need to begin a frantic search for new business is eliminated.

STRATEGIES, TIPS & TECHNIQUES TO APPLY

A salesperson can take as individual an approach to prospecting as they would like. Typically, the more creative the approach the more fruitful, but it is how a prospecting search is executed that counts. A systematic approach that clearly defines the ideal prospect works to provide the salesperson with a specific target to search for and a higher overall level of success. A broader, more general approach may produce more prospects, but also a higher level of frustration when they fail to qualify.

While prospecting activities are not limited to the following approaches, they represent the most common prospecting techniques used by salespeople.

Networking

Networking provides the highest quality of results, but must be actively and consistently utilized to yield a desirable number of prospects. Additionally, the salesperson needs to be well-versed in networking techniques for this approach to be fruitful.

Many salespeople will seek leads at networking events, but there are other networking sources such as actively soliciting leads and testimonials from within the salesperson's existing customer base. This can include trading leads with other salespeople within the company. When a salesperson receives a lead that is out of their area, they should forward it to the appropriate salesperson. Likewise, other salespeople should refer and share their leads.

Another approach is to network with other salespeople that are trustworthy and encountered on a regular basis and salespeople of equipment suppliers who use the product the salesperson sells.

Additional but often overlooked sources of referrals might include bankers, lawyers, consultants and accountants who have regular access to a number of companies.

Web-Based Search

The next best source of prospecting is to harness the power of the Internet—a tremendous advancement for salespeople. A great number of prospective businesses can be readily searched and reviewed in a relatively short period of time. Additionally, if salespeople take time to clearly define their search parameters, they should easily produce a quality list of prospects, while simultaneously accessing the information they need to approach these companies.

Physical Search

The physical prospecting search relies on traditional prospecting techniques such as searching phone books, directories, newspapers and trade journals. This tends to be tedious and time-consuming. The majority of information available in print is also generally accessible through electronic means.

'Chasing Smokestacks'

The final method, also a traditional prospecting approach, consists of "chasing smokestacks." This implies that a salesperson will physically search an industrial park or office building for prospective business. This approach is the most frustrating, time-consuming, expensive and ineffective.

The Best Approach

The best approach is typically a combination of all of the most common approaches. The key is for salespeople to identify the most productive mix for them, then closely match the results to their capabilities. Some individuals do very well at networking, while others have difficulty associating with other people at busy, active parties and events. The same may be true of Internet prospecting: some individuals are very comfortable with the computer while others will seek to use it as little as possible. Additionally, other creative methods not detailed above may be used.

POINTS TO PONDER — SOMETHING TO THINK ABOUT

1. What has been your most effective prospecting approach? What results did you experience after using it consistently?
2. What was your least productive prospecting approach? Why do you think it was unproductive?

TRAINING ACTIVITY — APPLICATION & ACTION PLAN

Determine the best prospecting approaches for you and the percentage of prospects you expect to identify using each method.

1. Prioritize the individual methods by the quality of prospects you expect to identify.
2. Finally, develop a prospecting plan based upon the methods you plan to use.
3. Create a timeline of when you plan to prospect and the number of prospects you hope to identify.

6

Identifying the Quality Prospect

Not all prospects are alike, and the best prospects may not necessarily be readily identifiable. After all, a book can't be judged by its cover. A successful prospecting strategy identifies the best and most likely prospects for the salesperson to maximize the use of their time and resources.

IMPLICATIONS — WHAT THIS MEANS TO YOU

Prospecting is one of salespeople's least favorite activities: it takes a great deal of effort to sort through potential customers, contact them and handle the subsequent rejection and frustration.

Much of this frustration can be minimized if salespeople take the time and effort to identify the parameters of their initial search. Most are aware of the concept of the sales funnel, where as an issue of simple mathematics a specific number of prospects will yield a certain number of rejections but also a specific number of appointments and then sales. However, the fact that salespeople have a limited amount of time in which to develop new business and create the desired level of sales is often used as an excuse for procrastinating when it comes to prospecting and cold calling. Most salespeople don't see the immediate return in prospecting that can be produced from other activities.

Salespeople do have the power of technology to maximize their ability to identify the best prospects with the least amount of time and resources. This also minimizes the frustration they experience when they initially contact the companies to determine their interest and desire or need for their product.

STRATEGIES, TIPS & TECHNIQUES TO APPLY

The key to identifying the best and most likely prospects lies in the time and thought a salesperson spends defining the parameters of their initial search. It is better to conduct a series of closely targeted searches than a broad search for potential customers. The following steps should be conducted to identify the most likely prospects:

Identify Parameters of Search

The most important step in identifying the best prospects is to establish the parameters of the search. Although the specifics have been detailed in previous lessons, a quick review is in order.

First, a profile of the ideal target company is created based upon an analysis of the salesperson's existing customer base. This profile describes the characteristics of the target company, including their industry and company type, application, use, volume, location and a host of other variables that describe the company. It is likely that several profiles can be developed based upon the product mix a salesperson is selling. Each individual profile results in a separate prospect search.

Once a profile is created, a series of keywords that will define the search parameters can easily be created. These key words will be used as the basis for a prospect search.

Filter

Once the keywords are identified, it becomes easier and more effective to use them with an Internet search engine. There are a number of powerful engines to choose from.

The power of the Internet will perform the initial filtering that in the past would have been done by hand. The resulting list of companies produced should closely match the parameters listed by the salesperson. Undoubtedly there will be companies or websites identified offering no potential that should be ignored.

The salesperson needs to physically filter through the resulting list of companies yielded by their search until a final list can be compiled.

Identify

It is important to physically visit each website identified by the search to identify the most likely prospects. Once again the target criteria should be applied to pre-qualify each prospect. As the salesperson reviews individual company sites, information may be downloaded or printed to create a file on each prospect for future use and reference.

Prioritize

The last step is for salespeople to compile a final list and then prioritize the most likely prospects based upon a desired classification system. The final list produced should include the most likely prospective customers for the salesperson to contact. As one works through the list, the potential will decrease, but the top of the list should be highly productive. This will maximize the salesperson's efforts and minimize the frustration of calling on companies who have little or no need for their products and services.

POINTS TO PONDER — SOMETHING TO THINK ABOUT

1. What search parameters have you used in your prospect identification in the past? How effective were they in selecting only the most likely prospects?
2. What has been the biggest frustration you have experienced in past prospecting activities?

TRAINING ACTIVITY — APPLICATION & ACTION PLAN

1. Using the four steps identified above, develop a target profile and conduct an Internet search for prospects.
2. Filter, identify and prioritize your list to compile a list of most likely prospects.

7

Qualifying the Prospect

Every sale takes a great deal of time and preparation. In fact, the success or failure of an individual sale is determined by the degree of preparation conducted by the salesperson before contact is made with a prospect. Most salespeople resist this concept as they would rather be in the field than researching the prospect and analyzing their situation, needs and how they can provide them with a unique value-added solution.

It doesn't make sense for a salesperson to invest in a prospect who has little or no potential of ever becoming a customer. Yet, many salespeople make a fatal assumption that most, if not all prospects, are automatically qualified. They have the tendency to short-circuit the qualifying process in an effort to land a quick sale. This often results in wasted time, lost orders and unnecessary objections. When this occurs, the salesperson must start over to determine if the prospect is truly qualified and has a genuine need for or specific interest in their product.

IMPLICATIONS — WHAT THIS MEANS TO YOU

One of the primary causes of prospect objections is the failure of the salesperson to adequately qualify. The foundation of a long-term customer relationship is laid in the qualifying stage. Experienced salespeople earn a prospect's respect by demonstrating their professionalism and expertise in taking the time to properly and adequately qualify them as potential customers. This means making the effort to discuss what the prospect needs and the solutions they are looking for. The priority should be to assist the prospect and not to make the sale. The salesperson needs to understand the reasons why the prospect is seeking specific solutions by asking thoughtful questions and doing a lot of listening.

A careful needs analysis at this point may cause the salesperson to lose some prospects who don't have a need but will solidify prospects who do. This is the purpose of qualifying.

STRATEGIES, TIPS & TECHNIQUES TO APPLY

Proper qualifying of a prospect goes beyond establishing a need for a particular product or service. A number of other factors must be considered and established prior to moving forward.

One of the primary factors that should be immediately established is the prospect's financial ability to purchase the product or service. During economic slowdowns, the salesperson must also determine whether the prospective buyer is budgeted for the purchase and if so when the funds will be available. In business downturns, many companies can still afford to make a purchase, but may choose not to make any new and major financial commitments until business conditions improve.

A prospect's ability to afford a product or service is often a sensitive issue. The prospect may consider their financial information confidential or they may fear they will be charged more than they are prepared to pay if they reveal this information.

Salespeople need to probe for a range that the prospect is comfortable with spending for their product or service. This provides them with the input they will need to craft a solution that falls within the proper limits.

The second primary factor a salesperson needs to identify is a list of all of the decision makers involved in the buying decision. Selling to a person who lacks purchasing authority only wastes the salesperson's time and resources. Purchasing committees make most major buying decisions. Salespeople need to identify all of the committee members, including their authority and responsibilities.

The third primary factor salespeople need to determine is the purchasing time frame the prospect will be following. Sales are often lost due to poor timing. Many prospects may be laying the groundwork for future purchases but delaying a final decision until the economy improves. Salespeople need to determine when the prospect plans to make the purchase and plan their sales strategy accordingly. However, due to the volatility of the economy, it may be productive to work with a prospect who is laying the groundwork for a future purchase. A sudden upturn can quickly lead to a buying decision.

As the salesperson qualifies a prospect, he or she needs to uncover the competitive situation and identify what if any other products the prospect is considering. A competitive comparison of these products will help the salesperson position him or herself with the prospect and verify their budget ranges.

The final stage of qualifying a prospect involves eliminating as many objections as possible by asking questions and soliciting feedback. Salespeople should think ahead and consider the most common objections they may encounter throughout the qualifying process. Proper qualification eliminates most objections by identifying specific needs and developing solutions based upon the information provided by the prospect.

Properly done, qualifying establishes a salesperson's professionalism and creates a firm foundation upon which to build future sales. Salespeople who properly identify and pre-qualify prospects by conducting a structured prospecting search will have developed sufficient information to make their qualification call a productive undertaking with little or no surprises. Thorough research enables salespeople to quickly identify the prospect's hidden needs, agendas and pressing issues. They will know exactly where to focus their questions and efforts.

While it may appear to take more time than most salespeople wish to invest in a sale, it is firmly established that a well-prepared approach to qualifying a prospect is the shortest path to building sales and developing relationships.

POINTS TO PONDER — SOMETHING TO THINK ABOUT

1. What additional factors do you feel you need to consider when qualifying a prospect?
2. What problems and pitfalls have you encountered by not adequately qualifying a prospect? Explain.

TRAINING ACTIVITY — APPLICATION & ACTION PLAN

1. Outline on a sheet a paper, the steps you take and the information you collect when you qualify a prospect.
2. Compare your qualification process against the strategies listed above and identify any gaps.
3. Develop a qualifying checklist that you can use with future prospects.

8

Identifying the Right Decision Maker

Selecting a prospect is relatively easy compared to identifying the right decision maker within the organization. Decision makers tend to mask their identity and form a wall of gatekeepers and screeners against unwanted interruptions.

IMPLICATIONS – WHAT THIS MEANS TO YOU

How and when a salesperson can identify the decision maker will have an impact on the success or failure of a sale. The best choice for a salesperson will vary from company to company and according to the product or service they sell. However, the higher in the hierarchy a salesperson can target their initial efforts, the better they will be able to reach the decision maker. Additionally, typically the higher the level a salesperson can sell at, the fewer competitors they will encounter.

There is one caveat to selling at higher levels. If the salesperson fails to convince the senior-level decision maker or is unprepared and unprofessional in their presentation, they risk losing the account at a level that will make it extremely difficult to recover. In this instance, the risk may be as great as the reward, underscoring the need to be totally prepared.

STRATEGIES, TIPS & TECHNIQUES TO APPLY

There is a hierarchy of decision making in most companies. Where the salesperson focuses their effort can make a tremendous difference in whether or not a sale will be made and the degree to which rejection and frustration will be encountered.

Buying decisions can be made at various organizational levels depending upon the complexity of the product and impact it will have on the company. Salespeople need to determine the level where decisions are being made about their products and services and focus their efforts accordingly. If they aim too high in the organization, decision makers won't give them the consideration; too low and they will need to fight layer by layer to arrive at the decision maker. The course of least resistance is to properly identify the level where the decision is made in the first place.

The common choices for a salesperson include the following individuals:

Purchasing Agents

Most salespeople will target their efforts at the purchasing agent since they are normally the most accessible. Unless the purpose is merely to get information, this is the worst place to begin. Purchasing agents typically act as screeners and gatekeepers. Most do not have the power to make the ultimate buying decision. Once a buying decision has been made, they may monitor the activity.

Additionally, salespeople will face the stiffest competition at this level, as this is where most of the competition will also focus their efforts.

If a salesperson is selling smaller, lower-priced items such as office supplies, the purchasing agent may be the best option, but any other type of product or service requires moving up the ladder to identify the decision maker.

Salespeople must be careful not to offend a purchasing agent since he or she also may be an influencer. The decision maker may seek their input when considering various vendors.

Product or Service Users

Product or service users are typically product evaluators and can influence the decision maker. They are worth fostering a relationship with, but typically will not be the actual decision maker.

Technicians

In some cases the salesperson will be dealing with engineers and other types of technical staffs. These individuals are often evaluators and influencers but not the decision makers. Their input is essential and they should be nurtured, but the salesperson will most probably need to focus their efforts at a higher level.

Managers

Identifying the right manager to make a purchasing decision can be a tricky process. Some may be screeners, influencers or ultimate decision makers. Certain managers will imply they have the purchasing authority when in fact they do not.

When initially qualifying an account, salespeople must clearly determine the role of the manager they are dealing with. If not properly identified, the salesperson can waste a great deal of time and face a large number of objections as the manager attempts to mask their true identity and buying authority.

The key is to define the level and the authority of the individual manager until the right manager is identified. This needs to be done discretely so as not to offend any lower-level managers and make an enemy of them.

Senior Executives

Senior executives, especially at the C Level (CEO, CFO, CIO, COO) are the best options but also the most difficult to reach. While normally well screened and protected from unwanted interruptions, they will have the ultimate purchasing authority. Due to the executive's lack of accessibility, the successful salesperson will have little competition.

Additionally, C level individuals are focused on the impact the salesperson's product or service will have on profitability rather than on features and benefits. The salesperson who wishes to sell at this level must be prepared to discuss the financial impact of their product in terms of return on investment and profitability.

Purchasing Committees

Many companies are turning to purchasing committees to make major purchasing decisions. These committees might include every one of the individuals listed above, including the decision maker. Often, the decision maker will mask their identity from vendors and rely on other members of the committee to gather information and give the appearance of being decision makers.

When a salesperson is faced with a purchasing committee, they need to find an individual who will champion them to the group while providing inside information on the identities, authority and agendas of the individual members.

POINTS TO PONDER — SOMETHING TO THINK ABOUT

1. How successful have you been in identifying and making contact with the right decision makers in a prospective customer's business?
2. Have you experienced frustration and rejection because you failed to identify the right decision maker? Explain.

TRAINING ACTIVITY — APPLICATION & ACTION PLAN

1. Examine your list of current prospects. Identify the specific level you are currently selling at for each prospect.
2. Identify the prospects where you are selling below the levels where the decisions are being made.
3. Determine the individual or individuals who you need to see and how you will gain access to them.

About the Author

Timothy F. Bednarz, Ph.D. is CEO of the American Management Development Group, Inc. For over 20 years he has researched, designed and authored hundreds of learning and development programs used by Fortune 1000 companies.

He is also the author of *Great! What Makes Leaders Great. What They Did, How They Did It and What You Can Learn from It* (2011).

Speaking Availability

Timothy F. Bednarz, Ph.D. is available for speaking engagements for your next meeting or association event. He can be contacted at 800-654-4935 or by e-mail at timothy.bednarz@majorium.com.

Bulk Sales

Bulk sales of this book or any other titles available from Majorium Business Press. Inquiries can be directed to sales@majorium.com, or by phone at 800-6654-4935.

Quick Order Form

Fax orders: 715-342-1118. Send this form.

Telephone orders: Call 800-654-4935 toll-free. Have your credit card ready.

Email orders: sales@majorium.com

Postal orders: Majorium Business Press, 2025 Main Street, Stevens Point, WI 54481, USA.

Please send the following books:

____

____

____

____

Please send more FREE information on:

❑Catalog ❑Speaking/Seminars ❑Mailing Lists ❑Consulting

Name: ____

Address: ____

City: __________________________ State: _____ Zip: __________

Telephone: ____

Email address: ____

Sales tax: Please add 5.5% for products shipped to Wisconsin addresses.

Shipping by air:

United States: $4.00 for first book and $2.00 for each additional product.

International: $9.00 for first book; $5.00 for each additional product (estimate).

Made in the USA
Monee, IL
08 November 2026

67382856R00026